Text copyright © Pat Thomas 2006
Illustrations copyright © Lesley Harker 2006
First published by Hodder Children's Books in 2006

This paperback edition published in 2007 by Wayland,
an imprint of Hachette Children's Books

Editor: Kirsty Hamilton
Concept design: Kate Buxton
Series design: Jean Scott Moncrieff

British Library Cataloguing in Publication Data
Thomas, Pat, 1959 –
My manners matter : a first look at politeness
1.Courtesy – Pictorial works – Juvenile literature
I. Title
395.1'22

Printed in China

ISBN 978 0 7502 5284 3

Hachette Children's Books
338 Euston Road,
London NW1 3BH

My Manners Matter

A FIRST LOOK AT POLITENESS

PAT THOMAS
ILLUSTRATED BY LESLEY HARKER

WAYLAND

Have you ever heard someone say 'mind your manners'? Do you know what that means?

Our manners are the ways we treat others and act in public. Good manners show both kindness and respect to people you know – and to people you may not know.

When we have good manners we are polite
and we follow certain rules that make us more
enjoyable to be around.

People can tell if you have good manners by
the way you talk and by the way you act.

Good manners are like magic,
because when we are well
behaved it makes special
things happen.

Please?

Saying 'please' can make
others more willing to help us.

Saying 'thank you' makes other people feel good about what they have done.

Saying 'I'm sorry' when you have hurt someone can make both of you feel happier.

Lots of people think it's important to behave
well only on special occasions.

But really we should be practising good
manners every day, with everyone we meet.

Opening the door for someone else, congratulating the winning team or offering your seat to someone who is not as strong or as healthy as you are all good ways of showing what good manners you have.

So is not making a noise when others are trying to work or listen.

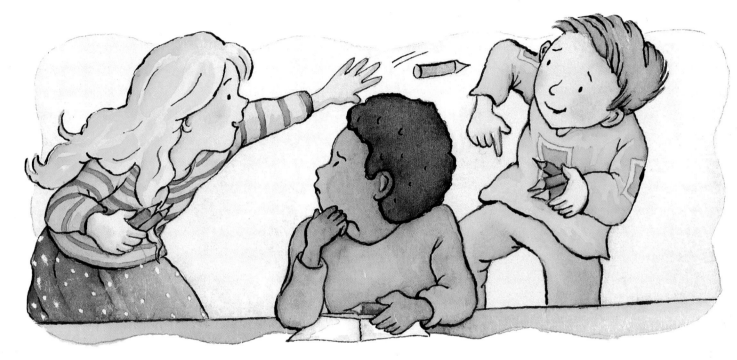

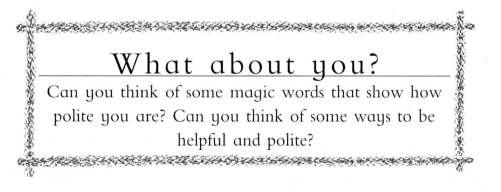

What about you?

Can you think of some magic words that show how polite you are? Can you think of some ways to be helpful and polite?

How you behave at the table or on the phone is also important.

Sitting up straight, not talking with your
mouth full, and saying thank you for
a nice meal is always polite.

So is speaking clearly and
politely on the phone.

Some people are always being rude. They think people will respect them if they act tough and inconsiderate. It's hard to be polite to them, but try anyway.

Rude people are often very lonely people –
nobody likes to spend time with them because
they hurt other people's feelings and take the
fun out of everything.

A long time ago people had
many different ideas about
what good manners were.

Children were considered rude if they spoke to an adult without being asked to, or if they didn't stand up every time their teacher came into the room.

Some of these ideas seem silly now and lots of ideas about being polite have changed over the years.

But some ideas are always good – like taking turns, not pushing or shoving, playing fair, asking before you take something and covering your mouth when you sneeze.

What about you?

Why do you think it's important to practise good manners? Can you say why it is a good idea to ask before you take something that doesn't belong to you?

People from different cultures may have
different rules about manners.

Older people may also have been brought up
with different ideas about what it means to
be polite and how children should behave.

It's important to try to understand these differences and show respect for them.

It doesn't matter whether there are just two of you playing or working together, or whether you are in a big group in the classroom or the playground.

Manners are important wherever you are
because being polite makes working and
playing together more enjoyable for everyone.

HOW TO USE THIS BOOK

Even though character building is a hot educational topic, manners generally receive little attention in schools. With growing demands on teaching time, manners and etiquette are usually abandoned in favour of teaching the 'three R's'. While manners today are definitely more casual than in the past, if parents want their children to get by in 'polite society' they need to make the effort to teach politeness and respect in a deliberate, intentional way.

Explain to your children why manners are important. They need to hear from you that these rules are important not simply as codes to live by, but as acts of kindness and consideration for others.

Teaching your children manners also gives them life-long survival skills such as self-esteem and self-confidence. Your children learn manners (along with many other character traits) from you. Do your best to speak politely and always treat them and others with kindness and consideration. Teach children to practise common courtesy by writing thank-you notes for gifts, sending thoughtful letters or emails to friends and relatives, and remembering birthdays, holidays and those who are elderly or ill.

Social skills are complex and with young children it's best to take a step-by-step approach. The first lesson for all children should be using time-honoured 'magic words' such as "please" and "thank you". Gradually add more examples such as "you're welcome" and "pardon me?" and "may I…" For table manners, work on one or two at a time. On the telephone encourage clear "hellos" and "good-byes" first, then teach asking the caller to "Please wait a minute while I get my dad." Teach children to take messages.

Teachers can help by instigating discussions about everyday manners and ways to handle ourselves in tricky situations. Ask children to come up with solutions to problems such as: If someone is rude to you how do you respond? If someone gives you a present that you don't like what should you say?

Schools provide ample opportunities for children to practise good manners. When a theatre company comes to the school and puts on a play, or the local police officer or firefighter comes to talk to the children, ask the students to write thank you emails or notes and say what they enjoyed about the visit. If you have a school fair or cake sale, have the children write short notes to thank the organisers – often busy parents who could use some appreciation.

BOOKS TO READ

'Excuse Me – Learning About Politeness'
Brian Moses, Mike Gordon (Wayland, 1998)

'Madeline Says Merci: The Always Be Polite Book'
John Bemelmans Marciano (Puffin, 2006)

'Oops! Excuse Me, Please! and other mannerly tales'
Bob McGrath, Tammie Lyons (Barron's Educational
Series. 1998)

'The Bad Good Manners Book'
Babette Cole, (Puffin Books, 1997)

'Manners Can Be Fun'
Munro Leaf (Universe Publishing, 2004)

RESOURCES FOR ADULTS

'Multicultural Manners: New Rules of Etiquette for
the 21st Century'
Norine Dresser (Wiley, 2005)

'Teaching Your Children Good Manners: A Go
Parents! Guide'
Lauri Berkenkamp, Steven C. Atkins
(Nomad Press, 2001)

www.emilypost.com
Web site of the Emily Post Institute, founded by the
doyenne of manners in America. This site provides
answers to your everyday etiquette questions and
manners issues.